Hittites

The True and Surprising History Of The Ancient Hittite Empire

©Copyright 2016 by From Hero To Zero - All rights reserved.

The follow eBook is reproduced below with the goal of providing information that is as accurate and reliable as possible. Regardless, purchasing this eBook can be seen as consent to the fact that both the publisher and the author of this book are in no way experts on the topics discussed within and that any recommendations or suggestions that are made herein are for entertainment purposes only. Professionals should be consulted as needed prior to undertaking any of the action endorsed herein.

This declaration is deemed fair and valid by both the American Bar Association and the Committee of Publishers Association and is legally binding throughout the United States.

Furthermore, the transmission, duplication, or reproduction of any of the following work including specific information will be considered an illegal act irrespective of if it is done electronically or in print. This extends to creating a secondary or tertiary copy of the work or a recorded copy and is only allowed with express written consent from the Publisher. All additional right reserved.

The information in the following pages is broadly considered to be a truthful and accurate account of facts and as such any inattention, use, or misuse of the information in question by the reader will render any resulting actions solely under their purview. There are no scenarios in which the publisher or the original author of this work can be in any fashion deemed liable for any hardship or damages that may befall them after undertaking information described herein.

Additionally, the information in the following pages is intended only for informational purposes and should thus be thought of as universal. As befitting its nature, it is presented without assurance regarding its prolonged validity or interim quality. Trademarks that are mentioned are done without written consent and can in no way be considered an endorsement from the trademark holder.

Introduction

Congratulations on downloading this book and thank you for doing so.

This book, Hittites: The True and Surprising History Of The Ancient Hittite Empire, is a synopsis of the history, culture, and main contributions of the Hittites, a vast and impressive empire that was based in present-day Turkey. Their contemporaries included Ramses the Great and King Tut. They were friends with the Trojans and created correspondence regarding the Trojan War with other kings of that era. The queens were as powerful as the kings, signing treaties and making laws.

Hittite history is broken into four periods:

- The Pre-Hittite Hattis
- The Old Kingdom
- The Middle Kingdom
- The New Kingdom

Each of these ages are discussed, including a list of the kings and their relevant contributions to the kingdom. There is a timeline at the end of the book that lists the kings, their years' of rule, and major events that affected the empire.

We also evaluate the importance of the Hittites, and their presence within the Iron Age.

Finally, we list the legacy of the Hittites, their best accomplishments, and their remarkable ideas.

The most valuable contribution of the Hittites was the enormous and well-preserved library of contemporary documents of their complete chronological history, enabling us a window into their world. Come with us to see the Hittite Kingdom up close and personal.

There are plenty of books on this subject on the market, thanks again for choosing this one! Every effort was made to ensure it is full of as much useful information as possible, please enjoy!

Table of Contents

Introduction 4

Chapter 1: Beginnings.. 7

Chapter 2: Before the Old Kingdom of the Hittites 15

Chapter 3: The Old Kingdom 17

Chapter 4: The Middle Kingdom...36

Chapter 5: The New Kingdom 38

Chapter 6: The Hittites and the Iron Age............................... 53

Chapter 7: The Legacy of the Hittites..................................... 55

Chapter 8: Hittite Society.. 59

Chapter 9: Hittite Timeline 66

Conclusion 70

Chapter 1:
Beginnings

Who Were the Hittites?

The Hittites lived in Anatolia before 1700 B.C.E., developing a culture that incorporated both the Hatti and the Hurrian practices. Their empire was equal to that of Egypt, and was so threatening to them they eventually had to make a peace pact.

The Hittites are written about in the Old Testament (Christian Bible), or the Hebrew Tanakh, as the enemies of the Israelites and of God. Beginning at the conquest at Canaan, the Hittites or Hethites, are listed as one of the four nations that were never overcome by the Israelites.

According to the Book of Genesis, Chapter 10, the Hittites were the descendants of Noah, through Ham, then Canaan, and then Heth. (Gen 10:1-6)

In Genesis, Chapter 23, Abraham bought a cave from Ephron the Hittite. The cave was located at Machpelah to be used for the burial of family members, firstly, his wife Sarah. (Gen 23:10)

Esau had two wives that were Hittites. (Gen 26-36)

Ahimelech and Uriah, King David's generals, are Hittites. Uriah was killed in battle so that David could marry Uriah's wife, Bathsheba. (1 Sam 26:6 and 2 Sam 11:3)

King Solomon had several Hittite wives, and received tribute and trade with the kings of the Hittites. (1 Kings 11:7 and 2 Chron 1:17)

Elisha discusses the kings of the Hittites. The capital city of Israel, Samaria, was overtaken by the Syrian army. Israel had given up the idea of surviving the battle when they heard the approaching troops. The Syrians retreated. The prevailing thought was that the king of Israel had hired the Hittites to fight the Syrians and they fled. (2 Kings 7:6)

Ezra made the last reference to the Hittites. He stated that the Hittites were intermarrying with the Israelites. (Ezra 9:1)

The modern name of which they are referred is the Hittites, based on both the Bible and the Amarna Letters of Egypt. The letters refer to a Kingdom of Kheta, also referred to as the Kingdom of Hatti. They referred to themselves as the Nesili.

Scholars agree the Old Kingdom was between 1700-1500 B.C.E. and the New Kingdom, named the Hittite Empire, was from 1400-1200 B.C.E.. What is questionable for scholars is the Middle Kingdom, a period of 100 years. These years were considered the "Dark Ages" of the Bronze era, a murky time with few records or noted accomplishments.

Their Appearance

According to records, the Hittites were Indo-Europeans. Their skin had a yellow cast, their hair was black, their eyes were very dark, and their nose was long and pointy. Their faces were square shaped and they had high cheekbones.

They had two types of hats, a skull-cap, or a tall cone-shaped headpiece. They had a type of snow shoe that looked to be more of a ski with a topped leather footpiece. They also had skin moccasins.

Their clothing was brightly colored, made with rich natural dyes. The women wore long robes, as did the priests. The men wore long tunics, tall boots, but their knees were uncovered. The men often wore cloaks. The weapons on a well-dressed man included a dirk, a spear, a bow, and sometimes a battle ax. All of the weapons were made of iron, to the envy of the enemy nation states.

The Kings

The kings had many functions, including the duties of priest, ruler, judge, and the commander-in-chief of the military. The kings were surrounded by a retinue of servants and protectors, much like rock stars of today. The kings had just as much entanglements and intrigues as movie stars, often possessing both a wife and a harem.

The Cabinet members of the kings were chosen first, from family, then from friends, and finally from the nobility.

Cultural Practices

The Hittites were very fond of athletic contests. Each time there was a festival or a religious ceremony, contests of abilities were also observed. The favorite contest was the archery competition, held in front of the king. The winner of the contest was awarded a bottle of the king's wine by the king. The loser of the contest had to serve water to the remaining contests while naked.

There were stone lifting contests, shot put (with stones), and foot races. The winner of the contests usually won a prized livestock, often a bull or a pregnant cow.

The Armies

The armies were comprised of nobles, royal family members, citizens of the country, and career soldiers. Slaves and mercenaries were not allowed to serve in the military. The Nobles liked to serve because of the looting and the possibility of acquiring prisoners of conquest to work on their estates. The royal family members were the higher ranking officers. The citizens and the career soldiers shared barracks in Hattusa; people from the same region bunked in the same room so they could share their language.

The Story of the Tablets

Hattusa was annihilated around 1200 B.C.E. The walls surrounding the city were an inadequate defense against the neighboring nations. However, the Hittites were set on relaying the history and chronicles of their Empire in a written form of their own cuneiform. The discovery of the tablets that proved the historical existence of the Hittites changed the view of the Ancient World.

Archaeologist Charles-Felix-Marie Texier was searching in central Anatolia for the ruins of Tavium, a Roman settlement. He began to ask the local townspeople if there were any ruins nearby that had not been investigated. One of the locals in the town of Bogazkale told him to look in the hills overlooking the town.

Texier found a site with a four-mile perimeter wall that ran ¾ of a mile crossways. He could see the stones of a large foundation in the ruins. He knew this wasn't Tavium, but he wasn't sure what he had found. He did not realize he had just stumbled upon Hattusa, the capital city of the Hittite Empire.

About one mile from the ruins he saw an inscribed rock, with a cuneiform that he could not translate.

These same cuneiform recordings were seen on a rock discovered at Hamath, 350 miles south of Hattusa. J. Augustus Johnson travelled to Hama to locate the rock discovered by Burckhardt in 1809. They found that rock, attributed to Burckhardt, and three more. They had a local painter draw impressions of the rocks because the local Muslim tribes would not allow them to be touched or moved. The paintings were seen by Wright and Green, who travelled to Hamath in 1872, hoping to copy the inscriptions to work on translations.

The local citizenry were suspicious of the inquiries of Wright and Green, and so they lied about the rocks. Believing they were a rheumatism cure, they did not want to divulge the source of the magic healing stones. Wright and Green did not give up, and finally found a local man who knew of an inscribed stone. Indeed, it was embedded into the wall of his house!

Realizing there were more than just one stone, official documentation was presented to ask the Istanbul Archaeological Museum to take possession of all the stones located in Hama. The people of Hama protested in the streets and blocked the removal of the stones. Subhi Pasha, the Minister of Public Education, interceded by sending troops to protect the stones. The stones were found in homes and on the hillsides. One was enormous and took 50 men to move it one mile to the storage facility.

A meteor shower occurred that night, which was interpreted as an evil omen to the people of Hama. They believed the gods were angry that the stones were being removed. Minister

Pasha told the people that, on the contrary, the gods were happy the stones were being carefully preserved, as evidenced by the meteor shower that presented no harm to the people.

Wright and Green made casts of the stones, which were afterwards referred to as "Hamathite cuneiform," after the name of the city in which they were discovered. The stones went from a scarce commodity to an overabundance as they turned up all over the region. One stone was found at Aleppo and another at Carchemish, by the Euphrates River.

At separate times and in separate locations, the missionary Wright and Archibald Henry Sayce realized that the Hamathite cuneiform was written on all the collections of the mysterious stones. In 1880, Sayce announced at a Society for Biblical Archaeology meeting that the stones were carved by the Hittites. This tie to the biblical people peaked the interest of the society and the public.

Dr. Helmuth Bossert, a University of Istanbul professor, excavating at Karatepe in southern Turkey, found entryway columns that were written in both Hittite and Phoenician. These slabs were the key to translating the Hittite language.

The Hittites became less of a mystery when excavations started at Bogazkale, Turkey, the previous site of Hattusa, the capital city of the Hittite Empire. In 1905 Hugo Winckler found a cache of hidden tablets and fragments of writings. These tablets, carved by the Hittites, recorded an extensive history of events on clay that had been preserved through the ages.

Archeologist Winckler excavated 10,000 clay tablets from the archives of the royal library, a small fragment of the entire collection of more than 25,000 written tablets. It took until

1916 before Archibald Sayce and Bedrich Hrozny deciphered the texts so that we could see the chronology and culture of the Hittite people.

Where Did the Hittites Originate?

Anatolia is 1,000 miles across the diameter, from east to west, and 400 miles across from the north to the south. Asia Minor, as it was called by the Romans, was a constant battlefield throughout the ages. Because of the vast migration of peoples along this section, there is a wealth of archeological ruins available for study of the ancient tribes.

Before the Hittites were the Hatti. The Hatti occupied a kingdom in central Anatolia that was very sophisticated, made up of city-states. The Hatti claimed the cities of Alacahoyuk, Hattus, Marmatlar and Horoztepe.

Anatolia was also known as the "Land of the Hatti" and dates back to Sargon the Great, 2350-2150 B.C.E.

The Hatti people first appeared at the edge of the River Kizil Irmak in present day Turkey. The area was heavily wooded so their homes were built of wood. They traded timber and ceramics, tilled the soil and planted grains. They raised sheep, trading the wool for goods and also spinning and weaving garments and blankets.

Their religion was worship of the female goddess; everything in nature is sacred and possesses the Spirit of Goddess. It is speculated that they were more vegetarian in their diet and rarely consumed meat.

Anatolia was a coveted area because of the rich minerals in the region; there were deposits of copper, silver, iron and gold. Many battles were fought in Anatolia to try to possess the metals, especially iron, which gave a fighting advantage to the warriors in battle.

The Hatti began trading with Sumer; this lucrative export business brought Anatolia to the attention of Sargon the Great. Hatti established their capital as Hattusa, on the top of a hill. This was a well fortified fortress that was defensible from all sides. When Sargon the Great attacked the city, after destroying Ur, he marched on Anatolia but was unsuccessful in overcoming the fortress on the hill.

Sargon passed his antipathy and desire for Hattus to his grandson, Naram-Sin. Naram-Sin also attacked Hattus and King Pamba, but failed just as miserably as his grandfather. The Hatti people continued to flourish until the invasion of the Hittites.

This time when the Kingdom of the Hatti was attacked they lost, and the Hittites took over. King Anitta burned the city of Hattusa to the ground. King Annita was so angry with the Hatti that he cursed the ground and any future people that would try to rebuild the city.

Chapter 2:
Before the Old Kingdom of the Hittites

The Kings that descended from the Hatti were:

- Pamba
- Pithana
- Piyusti
- Annita
- Tudhaliya
- PU-Sarruma

Little is known of the earliest kings, although there are a few records written in cuneiform to give us information.

Pithana

King Pithana, also referred to as Pitkahanas, made his base of operations at Kussara. He was a well-known conqueror, expanding the Hatti and Hittite kingdom across Nesa (Kanesh).

King Pitkahanas passed his legacy to his son Anitta.

Anitta

King Anitta brought down the city of Hattusa and moved the capital to Nesa. There the capital stayed for 100 years, until the time of Hattusili I.

During the reign of King Anitta there was a usurper to the throne.

Piyusti

Piyusti challenged Anitta on two different occasions and both times Piyusti was defeated. In the second battle, Piyusti and his soldiers were located in the town of Salampa. Piyusti and his men did not challenge King Anitta again.

Tudhaliyas

Tudhaliyas took the throne but was an unremarkable king, with the exception of his heirs. He was the great-grandfather of one of the most renowned kings, Hattusili I. Tudhaliyas was also attributed to be Tidal, King of Nations, Genesis 14:1 and 14:9, who joined Chedorlaomer in the attack against the rebels of Canaan. Tudhaliya left his command to PU-Sarruma, his son.

PU-Sarruma

PU-Sarruma had ungrateful sons that turned against their father and his agents. Because of their attitude and behavior, he name Labarna as his heir. This was a problem for Papahdilmah, the next son in succession to the throne. He, and his servants plus the king's chief officers, rallied against the king, and took over the throne.

Chapter 3:
The Old Kingdom

The Old Kingdom, 16th to the 15th Century, B.C.E.

- Labarna I
- Hattusili I
- Mursili I
- Hantili I
- Zidanta I
- Ammuna
- Huzziya I
- Telipinu

Labarna I

The Hittites list Labarna as their first king; his wife's name is Tawannannas. As the years go by, other kings and queens are called by the same name and it appears as the personal names became grafted into titles.

Labarna was named by his father-in-law to be king but he struggled constantly with Papahdilmah. As many times a Papahdilmah challenged his appointment, Labarna would overtake Papahdilmah and emerge the victor. Labarna never forgot the challenge, and passed his attitude of enmity to his son, Hattusili I.

We don't know how popular Papahdilmah would have been as the king, because he was never really there. In his mind and the considerations of his cohorts he was the rightful heir and king, but the rest of the kingdom was very happy with Labarna and his reign. His name was so respected that the future kings would call themselves Labarna, like the Roman emperors would name themselves "Caesar".

Labarna was a great warrior, and expanded the kingdom to include north, central and southern Anatolia. These lands became the foundation of the Great Hittite Kingdom.

Labarna I began the golden era of the Hittite reign of power. He was known as the king who united the people, his son, his brother, his relatives, the troops and even his in-laws all lived in unity. The land claimed by the Hittites was small at first, but through the campaigns of Labarna I they grew to be considerable.

He would lead a raid on a neighboring city-state, emerge victorious, then retreat back to Nesa to enjoy the spoils. He continued to gather real estate, while also incorporating the people and the culture into the Hittite fold.

Labarna I expanded the reach of the Hittites to border the Black Sea and the Mediterranean Sea. Labarna stated he sent his sons to rule seven sections of the lands of the Hittites, Hupisna, Tuwanuwa, Nenassa, Landa, Zallara, Parsuhanta, and Lusna. These were all inland properties of the Hatti. Under Labarna, the city-states all prospered. The bordering states did also, but they were not under the control of his sons.

After Labarna I, the reach of the empire extended into Arzawa. This was a significant rivalry for the Hittites, and would continue to stymie them at every turn. Arzawa was the only western kingdom that was as large and powerful as the land of the Hittites.

Hattusili I

Hattusili I became king after Labarna, although Hattusili I was the adopted son of Labarna, and also a nephew to his wife, Tawannannas. In the first year of his reign he stayed within the local region, attacking only smaller places in Cappadocia and the surrounding areas. He continued the military conquest pattern of his predecessor, Labarna I.

Within Anatolia, Hattusili I attacked first the city of Sanawitta. He wasn't able to capture the city-state. In his wrath, he destroyed the lands and the garrisons, also defeating the troops. He continued on this route and moved to Zalpa, which he destroyed. He obtained three four-wheeled chariots with flat beds, called MADNANU-chariots, that he dedicated to Arinnidu, the Mother Goddess of the Sun. In addition, he also donated one silver ox and a silver fist to the Storm God, and more booty he dedicated to the Goddess Mezulla.

The second year of his reign he began to move into his power. He moved his troops into northern Syria to attack the city of Alalah. The strategic location of Alalah overlooking the eastern end of the Belen Pass over the Nur Mountains by Cilicia. Alalah was commanded by Ammitaqu, who had built a palace within the city. Hattusili sent his troops to overcome the city and burn down the palace. In their exuberance they continued to burn the city to the ground. Satisfied with his loot and the leveling of the city, Hattusili moved on to the city of Urshu. (The following is a personal account from the journal of Hattusili that has been preserved through the centuries.)

Hattusili stationed his troops in the city of Lawazantiya, from which he surveyed and commanded the attack against Urshu. King Hattusili summoned two of his senior officers, Sanda and Mananiya. Both of these officers have failed the king previously and they were now being chastised for their offenses. The king told the officers that if they will fulfill specific tasks he will pardon their offenses.

The officers, eager to remove themselves from the bad temper of the king, agreed to do whatever was necessary to make the offense disappear from the memory of the king. The king instructed them to take a battering ram and strike the city walls to create an opening for the troops to enter.

Sanda and Maniniya returned sheepishly and reported to the king they had broken the battering ram in their attempt to storm the walls.

King Hattusili was furious, and yelled at the officers. He told them they were always the bearers of bad news. Then the king offered one more chance for a pardon.

The king instructed the men to build a different type of battering ram, one of the Hurrian type. (The Hurrian type of battering ram was constructed of a large beam hanging from a pendulum of ropes so that the ropes gave the beam momentum. The previously used battering ram was only a large beam that was carried by soldiers and pushed into the thin walls of the city.) He then told them to build up the earth leading to the city. (This was to move the battering ram up the ramp so that it would reach the walls.)

It would take all winter to build the battering ram and make the sloped earth ramp. Sanda was the manager of the project and reported to the king in Lawazantiya.

Sanda reported that as soon as Urshu fell their King would surrender into the hands of the Hittites. King Hattusili grew complacent.

Unfortunately, at that same time, the king of Kargamis was watching from the mountains with his troops.

Two of the Hittite soldiers, Nunnu and Kuliat, took money that was meant to be paid to the King. Nunnu was brought before the king and punished for corruption.

The King had Nunnu removed from his post, he was replaced by Sarmassu. The king wanted to warn Sarmassu not to do the same thing so he had the two men, Sarmassu and Nunnu, placed together in an oxen yoke. Then he brought Nunnu's father in law and stationed him in front of the two of them, and had him killed.

The king wanted to see that the men had been splattered with the blood from his brutal killing. He called the men to him. They had turned their tunics inward so they appeared clean before the king. The king cried out and asked where the blood was. The guards told the king the garments were turned inside out. The king required the men to wear the blood on the outside to remind everyone what happened when someone stole from the king.

(This story, written by the King, tells us that the entire family was held accountable for the wrongdoings of one. King Mursili II practiced this same principle in another story where a man's father in law was to be killed. The man asked to be killed with his father in law also, the king ordered it so, and both men were killed for the crime committed.)

King Hattusili was occupied with the events at Urshu but the Hurrians also had troubles brewing. During this period the Hurrians were involved in small fights among the nobles over land and territories. It was a civil war that distracted the kings from the presence of the Hittites just outside of their kingdom. King Hattusili became angry that his officers were aware of the situation, but no one took the initiative to mount an attack on the Hurrians when their defenses were distracted.

The King became very sarcastic and asked his officers if they had become so weak as to turn into water. He then said that if you had at least fallen on your knees in front of them you could have frightened him to death!

The officers responded to the anger of the King by singing war songs to incite the troops. They did not move the troops towards the Hurrians. The King is frustrated and orders the officers to lead the soldiers to the city gates, burn the gates down, and fight the Hurrians.

The officers said we will send eight times as many soldiers as you request but instead stayed in the camp and did nothing. The Hurrians attacked the troops and killed many of them.

This time the King told the officers to block the roads to the city with the chariots. The four wheeled cart was useful in this case because it commanded more space than the common two wheeled chariot. The King said to spy on the city and note who came and went through the blockade. Let nobody inform the enemies of our plans, the Hurrians, the city of Zaruar, Halap, or Zuppa.

The officers went back to the blockades but it was futile. One of the spies came to the King and reported that a servant of the king of Halap had moved in and out of the city on five separate occasions, that the kind of Zuppa's servant was in the city at that time, and that soldiers from Zaruar moved in and out of the city at their leisure. He further reported that the king of Urshu had a servant that was bring food and supplies to the Hurrians to bribe them to help Urshu fight the Hittites.

From this section of the journal we have learned the Hittites employed spies and scouts and anticipated that the enemy would do the same. We read of the evolution of the battering ram from just a timber that may have been sharpened to a propelled device that used momentum. The change of the style of the battering ram instituted a change in the fortifications of the city; now the city walls that were thinly built to mark the boundaries of the city-states were modified. The new style of fortress walls were much thicker to withstand the momentum of the new style battering ram.

Bribes were a common form of troop recruitment to entice a soldier to change sides during a battle. King Hattusili also demonstrated the importance of closing all the entrances and exits to the place under siege, because of spies and intelligence gathering.

King Hattusili was not successful in the Siege of Urshu. The King moved forward, attacking Ikakali and Tashiniya to end the year with a victory.

Hattusili's third year of his reign was rife with enemies pressing the borders. After he established that he was the rightful king and leader, he began to have border skirmishes. The first to challenge his authority and real estate holdings was Arzawa, a very large kingdom on the south and west part of the peninsula. As Hattusili moved his soldiers toward Arzawa, he left his south and southeastern borders unprotected. Herein came the Hurrians, to close the gap and claim the territory.

His march to capture Arzawa was a disaster. He didn't capture any territory and his only spoils of war were cattle and sheep. His soldiers lost faith in his leadership and deserted him.

The Hurrians moved in and overtook everything but Hattusa. The outer kingdom lands rebelled and moved out from under Hattusili's thumb.

Hattusili tried to regroup. He first attacked Nenassa, whose people were so frightened from his previous reputation, and unaware of his current low circumstances, opened their gates of the city and surrendered to him and his officers without even firing an arrow.

Hattusili moved against Ulma in the south; he overtook that city, destroyed it, and then left it empty. He moved on the city of Sallahsuwa in the south. That city was in the midst of a civil war and the citizens obligingly set their own city on fire and offered allegiance to Hattusili. Hattusili returned victorious to Hattusa.

The Hurrians entered Mesopotamia and Syria from the northern borders and challenged Hattusilis for the rights. Hattusilis moved again from his attack against Arzawa, to go in the opposite direction to counterattack the Hurrians. He spent the next two years running from the northern borders to the southern borders fighting first against Arzawa, and then against the Hurrians.

King Hattusili started a six month campaign to overcome Sanahuitta, on the north side of Hattusa. After six months of onslaught, he destroyed the city. He moved from there to the city of Parmanna, which was one of the leaders of the coalition that was attacking the Hittites. The city surrendered to him at the gates. He left that city and moved on to Alahha, which he destroyed like he did Sanahuitta.

In his last military year of expansion, he went back to fight the Hurrians in Northern Syria. This time he had support in the form of extra troops from Aleppo.

King Hattusili led his troops into battle at the city of Zaruna, extinguishing the city. He took his army to Hassu, a city occupied by the Hurrians. Hammurapi II, the king of Halap, sent his commander of the troops, Zukrasi, and the chief of the Umman-manda armies, Zaludi, to the city of Hassu to fight against the Hittites. Hattusili's army ravaged both battalions, the combined armies of Halap and Hassu, and crossed the Euphrates. King Hattusili annihilated the city of Hassu and looted the people and the town.

King Hattusili brought the loot back to Hattusa and dedicated some of the spoils to his Gods. He mounted an attack on Tawanaga. He was successful, took the king as hostage, and then cut off his head.

He swept into Hahhu, battling the armies stationed outside of the gates. It took three lengthy assaults before he finally tumbled the city. He brought back gifts for the Sun Goddess. He exulted to all who would hear, testifying that he crossed the Euphrates, fought the armies of Halap and Hassu, and conquered Hahhu. Sargon the Great couldn't even destroy Hahhu, but King Hattusili did.

Hattusili reduced Halap to a crumble, from which it never recovered, but in doing so Hattusili received a mortal wound while he fought. He made it back to Hatti but had serious doubts about Labarna's abilities to lead. Evidently Labarna did not show the proper concern for the health of the failing Hattusili.

Hattusili proclaimed in his letters that Labarna, who had been adopted as his son and trained at his right hand, now had become cold and distant. Labarna had not asked about his health or recovery from his severe wound and had not shed tears of grief regarding the oncoming demise of his adopted father. Labarna was giving too much heed to the counsel of his brothers, sisters, and most often, his mother. Hattusili nicknamed Labarna's mother "the snake".

King Hattusili became enraged and declared that Labarna was no longer his son. He issued an edict and banished Labarna to an estate, changing his status from son to a priest.

While searching for his successor from his deathbed, he had more problems within his family. His son Huzziya was listening to the murmurings of the Tappassanda noble family. They wanted tax exemptions, and bribed Huzziya to revolt against the rulings of his father. Hattusili slapped him down, but removed him from the list of the contenders for the throne.

In Hattusa, one of the daughters of Hattusili joined a conspiracy to move her son into the position of heir to the king. King Hattusili exiled her to an estate and removed that grandson out of the contender list.

Finally, in desperation, Hattusili chose his grandson, Mursili, to be his successor on the throne. Mursili was untrained and very young, so young that it was three years before he was allowed by his advisers to lead a military campaign.

Who Were Hattusili's Parents?

Hattusili's parentage is a mystery. Even though he was a great warrior, he was only the adopted son of Labarna and not expected to perform in his kingly duties as well as he did.

In his personal journal, Hattusili says that he is the nephew of Tawannanna. Why this is an important distinction is because of the right of the succession to the throne through the male lineage. However, there is one condition that changes the line of succession.

In the Hittite code it is explained that first the right of succession goes to the prince, a son of the king. If the prince does not exist, the son of the king's brother (or the second in line) should become king. If there is no prince, and no son's from the second in line, then an antiyant-husband from the first ranked daughter can become king.

From this statement we can derive that Labarna I was the son in law to PU-Sarruma, who was listed as married to a first ranked daughter. This implies that Tawannanna was the purveyor of the royal bloodline. Hattusili wanted to emphasize that he was of the royal bloodline. He was a son of a prince that was disinherited. Labarna took him in adoption as his son, which is the meaning of the term antiyant-husband.

It is probably that he was Papadhilmah's son, the one that contested Labarna being named to the throne.

We also wonder what happened to the rest of the sons of Labarna and Tawannanna. They were placed as managers over the seven city-states so we can expect there to be at least seven sons. Where were they when the throne was being contested? It is unlikely they would let others take what was rightfully theirs.

Now Hattusili had a double-edged sword by claiming his royal blood through Queen Tawannanna. She decided to retain her rule as the Great Queen, and so began to groom her true sons for the kingly position.

Hattusili declared that Tawannanna's name be struck from memory, and that no one should speak her name, or that of her children. When he removed the dowager queen from her throne he could now prepare his own sons to rule the kingdom.

Mursili I

Mursili I was a good choice for the ruler of the Hittites, but he was very young. He only reigned 30 years before he was assassinated.

Mursili chose for his first military campaign to avenge the death of Hattusili by attacking Aleppo. Mounting a forward launch against the city, he battered down the walls and defeated the Hurrian army.

From Aleppo he moved toward Babylon. Samsu-Ditana was the Amorite king of Babylon in occupation of the throne. Samsu-Ditana had been battered with skirmishes along the border of northwest Iran. The Kassites were picking battles along the edge of the kingdom, wearying the troops and the King with their constant aggravation.

Mursili and his army marched 500 miles, following the Euphrates River south to the capital of Mesopotamia. The city-state of Babylon was built on the east bank of the Euphrates River, 60 miles south of modern-day Baghdad. The city was ruled by Amorites, of whom the king was Samsu-Ditana, the last descendant of Hammurabi.

Hammurabi had created the Babylonian Empire, which stretched from Iran at the eastern border to Syria at the western edge. Babylon, the city-state, was considered the largest city in the world for this time period. It had grown from a modest town to a walled city with pyramidal tower, known as Etemenanki the ziggurat. The ziggurat is thought by scholars to be the tower of Babel, and Babylon the city of Babel.

In Hammurabi's era, the economy was stable, trade was abundant with bordering countries, and the rivers and canals were fortified and improved. His code was the first preserved written code of laws. Once Hammurabi died Babylon began to crumble. The city-states that thrived under Hammurabi in a unified form of government and economy began to splinter into local rivalries. Outsiders like the Hurrians, the Hittites, and the Kassites were a continual threat to the peace within the city.

It was during this uneasy upheaval within the Babylonian Empire that King Mursili moved towards the city-state. Turning southeast, the troops and the king moved into the Amorite territories, and overthrew the city of Mari, located in present-day Syria. Continuing in his mission, King Mursuli began a series of short raids upon the borders of the city. The city was weakened by the desertion of the Sumerian people; not only did they know longer supply troops to the king, they also no longer paid their tributes. This left the Babylonian king with less troops and little money to hire mercenaries. The infrastructure was weakened, the water was now impure, and the fields were overfarmed. The kingdom was falling apart on the inside but it still held the key for the trade routes.

The Kassites were still picking at the outer walls of Babylon also. The two kings made a pact, it seems. There is no specific written notation of the deal between them, but this is the remaining result.

King Mursuli and his men joined with the troops of the Kassite king, Agum-Kakrîme, and stormed the walls of the city of Babylon together. The city fell and was sacked, the king was deposed. As his trophy, King Mursili took the god statue of Marduk, signifying that the city was conquered and the god was no longer in power. King Mursili also took significant amounts of plunder, which became an obstacle to his peaceful reign. (Some scholars state that he also took large bundles of grain, as his crop growth was stunted by the volcanic ash clouds of the Thera eruption.)

King Mursili received word of a rebellion in his territory, so he turned immediately and began the 500 mile march back to Hattusa. Although he had never ruled in the city, he was given trade routes through the city that were to his advantage and he kept political control over northern Mesopotamia.

The invasion of the Hittites changed history.

- The record of the sack of Babylon was written down and recorded, dating the culture and kingdom to 1595 B.C.E.. This recording is considered crucial for correct dating of the Dark Age, of the Bronze Age.

- The Kassites took over the city, removed the dynasty of Hammurabi, and controlled the city for the next 400 years.

King Mursili passed through the Hurrian territory, where he encountered troops that wanted the statue of the god, and the booty that Mursili was carrying. He was detained by the Hurrians and engaged in battle. He made it through the territory returned to Hattusa.

He was showing off his bounty to Hantili, his cupbearer. Hantili's function as cup-bearer was to serve and taste all the king's foods and wines. It was a very trusted position as the danger of being poisoned was a tried and true method of murdering a king. Furthermore, Hantili was the brother in law to Mursuli. His wife was Harapshili, Mursili's sister.

Hantili and Mursili were admiring all of the gold, silver and trinkets that were brought from Babylon when Hantili started to envy the wealth and coffers of Mursili. Zidanta, Hantili's son in law, pulled Hantili aside and murmured in his ear. He remarked upon the extravagant riches that Mursili was enjoying. He then suggested that if the two of them murdered Mursili, Hantili and he could be living in luxury instead.

Hantili thought about this idea and conceded that he liked it. Zidanta and Hantili began to plot the murder of the king.

Hantili I

Hantili and Zidanta found a time that the king was unaware, and they killed him. Between them they agreed that Hantili would serve as the successor to the throne. The royal blood now was again following the matrilineal lines.

King Hantili reigned over the kingdom for 30 years. He continued some of the military campaigns but accomplished little else.

Hantili inherited a kingdom that was scattering. He had small conflicts all throughout the kingdom. His chief concern was maintaining control of Syria. He traveled to the Carchemish to lead a military rout against the Hurrians. It has not been recorded whether he was successful, but it is known that from here he turned back to Hattusa.

On the return trip he stopped at Tegarama, possibly modern-day Gurun, in Turkey.

Hantili began to mutter to himself with paranoia in his tone. He remembered his slaughter of his father in law, Mursili, that had honored and placed him in the most trusted position of the royal household.

He stated in his records (paraphrased),

"What have I done by listening to the suggestions of Zidanta? As soon as I sat on the throne, the gods have conspired against me to compensate for the injustice I have done to Mursili."

Hantili grew more paranoid, wondering who was waiting to kill him as he did Marsuli. He is quoted as saying (in the Proclamation of Telipinu 12)

"Will I be protected? The gods protected Mursili..."

Hantili returned to Hattusa and was immediately assassinated by Zidanta I.

Zidanta I

King Zidanta, having wearied of being the outsider, decided that Hantili had enjoyed the spoils and riches of kinghood long enough. After murdering Hantili, Zidanta killed Piseni, the successor to the throne, and Piseni's children and chief officers. He killed all of the rest of the potential heirs so that his placement upon the throne could not be challenged by bloodline succession. As we are married to Hantili's daughter, the royal bloodline continued through the females.

Zidanta reigned for ten years and was then assassinated by Ammuna, Zidanta's son. The royal bloodline now continued through the patrilineal line for the first time in two generations.

Ammuna

Ammuna, the grandson of Hantili I, was the most disastrous king of all. In his 20 year reign the kingdom declined and fell apart, almost completely destroyed. More of the outer regions rebelled against the apathetic king until there was more insurgence than unity. Ammuna was not a peacemaker or a diplomat, as the kings before him had proven to be.

Ammuna did lead a foray into Nesa, but the city never stayed under his reign. He was called back again to meet their challenge of his leadership. He also quelled insurrection in Šattiwara and Šuluki, the River Hulanna Land, Zalpa and Purušhanda, all located within the interior of the Hittite kingdom.

Ammuna watched as the vast empire fragmented into pieces of small territories. Ammuna died of natural causes, ironically, and was succeeded by Huzziya, the son of a secondary wife. He also had one daughter, named Istapariya.

Huzziya I

Huzziya I hired two assassins to murder the two legitimate sons, Tittiya and Hantili. His Chief of the Palace Guards, Zuru, was hired to find men willing to kill for a price. Zuru appointed Tahurwaili, a lesser member of his family and a Gold Spearman, to kill Tattiya and his family members. Taruhsu, a courier of the king, was hired to kill Hantili and his family. These were the older brothers of Huzziya I and the sons of the primary wife of Ammuna. He had now eradicated the successors and cleared his way to be seated on the throne.

Huzziya I was limited in his reign to only five years. He was replaced by a younger son of Ammuna, Telepinu, and then banished to an outer kingdom and eventually murdered.

Telipinu

The Hittite Kings Hattusili I and Mursili I moved freely what was called the Pyramus River in southern Turkey, proving their dominance over Cilicia and the Syrians. This made the northern cities of Syria impassable to the Hittites. They were forced to detour southeast to the Taurus pass. Telipinu wrote a treaty with Kizzuwadna's king, Isputakhsus, agreeing to relinquish his claim on Arzawa in order to be allowed to use the route through the Northern Cities.

Under Hittite control, King Sunassura II agreed to be a vassal state, a relationship which placed him under the management and leadership of the Hittites, paying a tribute and supplying troops at the command of the King. King Sunassura II was the last to sit the throne of Cilicia.

As important as the military accomplishments of Telipinu are the political laws and reformations he established.

- He created a law of succession to the royal throne.

- He required the nobles to be united in loyalty to the king.

- He required the nobles to follow a specific course of action if they disagreed with the King, rather than having him murdered.

- The punishment for criminals must be decided by the Supreme Court, called the pankus, which was the whole citizenry. This took the power from the hands of the king.

Telipinu is regarded as the last king of the Old Kingdom.

Chapter 4: The Middle Kingdom

Kings of the Middle Kingdom (15th century B.C.E.)

- Alluwamna
- Tahurwaili
- Hantli II
- Zidanta II
- Huzziya II
- Muwatalli I

Alluwamna

Alluwamna was the son in law of Telipinu, married to Hapapseki. Alluwamna should have been the next successor to the throne, but he was banished, along with his wife, to Malitashkur. The son of Alluwamna, who later became a king, was Hantili II.

Hantili II

Hantili was one of the sons of King Alluwamna, who received land from his father, as documented in a recorded land grant.

Zidanta II

He is speculated to be the nephew of Hantili II. His wife was Yaya. Zidanta signed a parity treaty with his peer, the Kizzuwatna king, Pilliya. This is the last parity treaty signed between a king of Kizzuwatna and a Hittite king.

His successor was Huzziya II.

Huzziya II

Huzziya II was killed by Muwatalli I, the head of the royal bodyguards. Muwatalli I then grabbed the throne for himself. His wife was named Summiri.

Muwatalli I

Muwatalli came into power by killing his older brother, Huzziya. He was then killed by the Chief of the Palace Servants, Himuili, and the Overseer of the Gold Chariot Fighters, Kantuzili.

Tudhaliya II

Possibly the same person as Tudhaliya I, scholars are not sure. The kings would change their names after a climactic event. The addition of a "y", "us", or even "s" on the end of the name was due to translation and clerical errors, so the names are all interchangeable. The numbering can be incorrect for the same reasons.

Chapter 5:
The New Kingdom

The Kings of the New Kingdom (14th through the 12th centuries, B.C.E.)

- Tudhaliya I
- Arnuwanda I
- Hattusili II
- Tudhaliya II
- Tudhaliya III
- Suppiluliuma I
- Arnuwanda II
- Mursili II
- Muwatalli II
- Mursili III
- Hattusili III
- Tudhaliya IV
- Arnuwanda III
- Suppiluliuma II

Tudhaliya (I, II, III)

Tudhaliya I/II/III was the son of Himuili, and the grandson of Huzziya II.

Suppiluliuma

It is agreed that Suppiluliuma was the greatest king of the Hittite Empire. He reigned for almost forty years, although pinpointing the specific dates of his reign is problematic.

Suppiluliuma brought the kingdom of the Hittites into one massive and cohesive unit that rivaled the Egyptian Dynasty. He expanded the city of Hattusa to comprise more than 300 acres, and extended the walls of the city to encompass the expansion. He increased the territory of the Hittite Empire at the southern and eastern borders through fighting. The northern cities of Syria surrendered at the sight of his approaching armies and agreed to submit to the Hittites' governance.

With Suppiluliuma in his full power, he turned his attention towards the kingdom of Mittani. Under the tutelage of Tudhaliya his father, Suppiluliuma had a great mind for tactics and military strategy.

Letters were carried from Suppiluliuma to the Pharaohs Amenhotep III and Akhenaten regarding the support of the Mittani kingdom. Egypt was an ally of the Mittani, but Pharaoh Amenhotep III decided to withdraw his support for King Tushratta of the Mittani. This was a bold step for Pharaoh Amenhotep III, because his wife, princess Taduhepa, was the daughter of King Tushratta. Going against both his wife and his father in law, Amenhotep III feared the security of his kingdom against the growing empire of the Hittites more than he did the disapproval and ire of his family.

In the power struggle over Washukanni, a treaty was written between King Tushratta and Artatama II, a relative of King Shuttarna, the previous king of Mitanni. Egypt, because of the treaty written upon the marriage of Amenhotep and Taduhepa, was honor bound to support Tushratta in the conflict. King Suppiluliuma, of the Hittites, gave his strength and armies to Artatama II.

Tushratta anticipated the battle turning into a victory when Amenhotep suddenly withdrew his troops. The desertion of the Egyptian armies gave Suppiluliuma an open door to the Mitanni kingdom. Suppiluliuma moved forward, unmindful of the departing soldiers of his now ally Egypt, and tried to mount an attack on Syria by the common route through the Taurus pass by way of Kizzuwadna. When this attack was unsuccessful, Suppiluliuma moved unconventionally to attack from the rear of Wassukkani, going down the Euphrates valley.

Suppiluliuma stepped through the door left open by the Egyptians and into the city of Washukanni, and pummeled it. Tushratta was assassinated by his successor son, Mitanni fell and came under the rule of the Hittites.

Amenhotep of Egypt died and Akhenaten came onto the throne. Akhenaten was not gifted as a military leader and Suppiluliuma I continued to push his forces deeper in the kingdoms and states of Egypt. He took Byblos with no defense from the Egyptians.

At this time Egypt was the principal power in central and southern Syria. The Egyptians actually had held the territory for so long they had no inkling that it could change hands. The boundaries were firmly held and carefully guarded. Egypt would give a strong fight to anyone that appeared to encroach on these territories.

Part of this area include the city of Kadesh. Suppiluliuma I avoided Kadesh because he didn't want to attract the attention of the Egyptian Empire. The King of Kadesh, acting on behalf of King Akhenaten, tried to stop the southern expansion of the Hittite territory. Unfortunately, he forgot to consult with the Egyptian Pharaoh before he took this action.

King Aziru and his son, Aitakama, aggressively attacked the Hittites, expecting the support and assistance of the imperial troops of the Egyptian Empire. He lost the battle and received no troops. Instead, he, the nobles of the city, and his son, Aitakama, were all carried back to Hattusa, and held hostage by the Hittites.

In their mercy, the Hittites returned Aitakama to the city of Kadesh, who ascended to the throne. The city of Kadesh was back under the Egyptian Empire. Or so it seemed. In actuality, King Aitakama was now in favor with the Hittites, and had swapped his allegiance while in the capital city. Aitakama started to recruit other kings to change their allegiance to the Hittites also.

Pharaoh Akhenaten mounted an attack on Kadesh but was turned back by the stronger army of the Hittites.

After Pharaoh Akhenaten died, his son Tutankhamun took the throne. King Tut sent his general Horemheb to fight the Hittites in order to curb their aggressiveness, but the army under Suppiluliuma I grew larger and stronger with each conquest.

As Suppiluliuma I moved west of the Euphrates River, the Northern Cities of Syria surrendered to his troops and came under his command. With only a small resistance from the king of Kadesh (because he was already his secret ally), Suppiluliuma I and his armies swept southerly almost as far as Damascus. The Egyptian allies all melted into the background as Suppiluliuma moved quickly and mercilessly across the territories. Nuhassi, Amurru, Aleppo and then Alalakh all were now possessed by the Hittites.

Suppiluliumas made a reversal and returned to the capital city, but left his son Telipinus the Priest to defend the Syrian vassal states.

Telipinus walked into an unforeseen circumstance. When the Mitannian king Tushratta was assassinated, King Artatama asked Assyria for a pact of defense against the marching Hittites.

Thinking his new territories were well under control by Telipinus, Suppiluliumas returned to Carchemish, and toppled the city after an eight-day onslaught. Suppiluliumas wanted the territory to create a buffer zone between the Assyrians and the Hittites. He used Wassukkani as his base of the buffer zone.

King Tutankhamun died in 1327 B.C.E., at the age of 19, from malaria and an infected broken leg. His widow, half-sister, and queen, Ankhsenamun, wishing for children, wrote to Suppiluliuma I and asked him to send one of his own sons for her to marry. She and King Tut had two stillborn daughters. She had stated in her letter that she did not want to be married to a servant, she could not rule by herself, and she wanted sons to succeed her when she died. All of those were excellent reasons to ask for a husband but she left out one important factor: she was being pressured to marry her grandfather, Ay.

Suppiluliuma I was suspicious, but determined that the letter was a true request from the Queen. He sent his son Zananza to be her husband and rule as Pharaoh. Zananza was murdered before he even reached the border of Egypt, possibly by Horemheb or Ay, because they didn't want someone foreign born on the throne. Ay had disposed of his competition in a way that would discourage the other kingdoms to offer a bridegroom to replace Zananza. Ay neatly wrapped up the package that would place him in the position of Pharaoh. Ay forced his granddaughter to marry him.

Suppiluliuma I became incensed and turned all of his military might against Egypt in retaliation. He conquered the rest of the Levant, an area that stretched the length of modern day Kansas and half the width. The Levant was framed by the Taurus Mountains, the Mediterranean Sea, the Arabian Desert, and Mesopotamia, a total of 4,000 square miles. Modern day cities and countries within the Levant include Cyprus, Lebanon, Israel, Palestine, Jordan, and Syria.

Suppiluliuma brought thousands of Egyptian slaves back to Hattusa; they were infected with the plague (smallpox) that endured for two decades.

Suppiluliuma I died of the plague that he brought back with the slaves from Egypt, along with a huge segment of the population of Hattusa.

Arnuwanda II

Arnuwanda II had spent his life being groomed for his reign by Suppiluliuma I. Unfortunately, he had no time on the throne because he also was infected by the plague. He died and was succeeded by his younger brother, Mursilli II.

Mursilli II

Mursilli II, being young and never trained for kingdom rule, was underestimated by all of the surrounding nations. All of the years he was watching his brother Arnuwanda II being groomed, he was learning. He had more of his father's military insights than expected. He turned to the border tribes that had been so annoyingly disobedient and brought them under submission by might. He secured his borders with troops, then began to pursue expansion.

His first problem to encounter was the buffer zone outpost in Wassukkani. The Assyrians invaded the small vassal kingdom, establishing a new frontier border with Syria at the Euphrates River.

Carchemish and Aleppo continued to support the Hittites so that Mursilis could turn his attention to the southwestern border of Anatolia, Arzawa. Arzawa, together with Mira, Hapalla, and Kuwaliya started a revolt against the Hittite rule. Mursilis quashed this rebellion by killing the King of Arzawa and placing Hittite governors to control and manage the several kingdoms that have revolted.

The northern territories were bordered by the Kaska people. They were a well organized tribe that used guerrilla tactics to constantly pick at the Hittites on the border territories.

Catching the "rebellious" attitude, Azzi-Hayasa, an eastern kingdom based on the Lycus River revolted also. The king, attending religious duties at Comana, sent a general to pacify the Azzi-Hayasa. His brother Piyasilis joined him at Comana, but then became ill and died. His brother was the king of Carchemish.

Piyasilis' death started another revolt in Syria; this time Mursilis led the imperial army himself into the battle and the rebellious people took heed and quieted.

Mursilis reigned for 25 years and left his kingdom with secure borders to his son Muwatalli II.

Muwatalli II

Muwatalli II is the Hittite King that fought Ramesses II at the Battle of Kadesh, called the greatest battle of the ancient world. He relocated the capital of the kingdom to Tarhuntassa, and he appointed his brother, Hattusili, as the governor of Hattusa.

The Battle of Kadesh

The specific date of the Battle of Kadesh is not for certain, somewhere between 1300-1275 B.C.E.. The Hittite army was patrolling in the area of Kadesh and came upon an Egyptian party that included Pharaoh Ramses II. The Egyptian division was caught by surprise, fought valiantly, and managed to retreat. The conflict ended in a draw.

The consequence of this skirmish was the weakened confidence of the Hittite army in relation to battles with Egypt. For Egypt, this battle began the fall of the 19th Dynasty and an end to their plans for expansion. It took 16 years for the two empires to make a formal peace treaty, so important the Egyptians inscribed the treaty on the walls of the Karnak temple.

Kadesh propelled the status of the Hittite Empire into one of a major military presence within the region, while at the same time, initiating the beginning of the end for both empires. Hatussa would fall by an invader speculated to be the Sea Peoples. Ramses III would defeat one invader army, but their battles with the Sea Peoples depleted their fighting resources.

The city of Kadesh was the physical boundary between the kingdoms of the Hittites and the Egyptians. Egypt had a long-standing trade agreement with Syria-Palestine. As their geographical next door neighbor, the timbers of the Syria-Palestine area had been their primary source for wood. The strategic Sinai Peninsula was coveted for their copper resources. Memphis, Egypt, became a major trade center, launching ships for trade all down the eastern coast of Greece and the Mediterranean. During this period of the Middle Kingdom of the Hittites, Egypt controlled the area of Syria-Palestine.

Egypt received the migration of the Hyksos, who built up enough forces to challenge the kinds of the city-states in Egypt. The ruled Egypt and Nubia from approximately 1674 to 1573. During their reign, they imported and adopted the horse and chariot, the compound bow, and the vertical weaving loom. They suppressed a revolt by Thebes but Ahmose I dislodged them from Egypt.

Removing the Hyksos only solved part of the military unrest during this era. The Hurrians were distantly related to the Hyksos. The kingdom of Mitanni had decreased the boundaries of the Hittites in the Syria-Palestine area; they were also in control of Assyria.

After 17 lengthy campaigns against the Hurrians, Thutmose III captured Kadesh. Egypt had subdued the Mitanni, but the Hurrians were the counterpoint to the Hittites. When Egypt concentrated its fighting forces against the Hurrians, the Hittites steadily increased their might, and therefore, their kingdoms. Now the Hittites were the main and serious threat to the Egyptian Empire. Egypt sought an alliance with the Mitanni, which was agreed upon and sealed with the marriage of Thutmose IV with a Mitannian royal princess.

Suppiluliumas challenged Mitanni at Wassukani, resulting in the flight of King Tushratta. Suppiluliumas moved his troops into Syria. Ramses II was now faced with a dilemma: he could challenge the Hittites in the hope that the constant battles and defenses were weakening the strength of the armies, or if they were strong, it was better to be on the offense instead of the defense when in battle for the homeland.

Ramses II believed the disease and plague that killed Suppiluliumas I and his son, Arnuwanda, had weakened the fighting armies of the Hittites. The plague had lasted 20 years, and killed many people, and challenged the health of the remaining citizenry. There was no reason to believe the army had been spared from the devastation of the plague.

In addition, the Hittite king Muwatalli had charged his brother, Hattusili, with conspiracy. This internal conflict took time and energy away from leadership of the imperial army by the king.

The last supporting argument for the weakened state of the Hittite empire was the defection of the allegiance of Prince Bentesina of Amarru. Ammarru was the buffer zone between the Hittites and the Egyptians. Officially, Pharaoh Ramses sent one army to Amarru for support. Unofficially he had plans to conquer Syria.

The serious divisions within the Hittite empire had long standing consequences. After the Battle of Kadesh, Hattusili welcomed Amurru and Prince Bentesina, just to aggravate his brother. He then arranged a marriage of one of his sons to a daughter of Prince Bentesina for spite.

The Empires Face Off

The Hittites and the Egyptians were both about 20,000 strong. The Hittites had a huge force equipped with chariots, 3,500, which were driven by 10,500 charioteers. Half or so of the troops were foreigners, conquered people that had been conscripted by the King into the imperial army. The Egyptians had four divisions of 5,000 infantry each, and four sets of 500 chariots, one for each division.

The Hittites and the Egyptians both were using the newer spoked wheel on the chariots.

This made the chariots lighter, faster, and easier to manipulate. The two empires employed different tactics. The Hittites manned one driver and two soldiers per chariot, one to drive the chariot, and two to fight the enemy; one soldier held a shield for defense, the other soldier fired the arrows at the opposing troops. The Egyptians had one driver and one archer. This sent less fighters, but they were faster.

Ramses II led the Egyptian army. He lacked experience in battle, but his troops had participated in many conflicts. Muwatalli commanded the Hittites.

Ramses had very few spies and was unfamiliar with his territory. His intelligence regarding the land and geography, or the location of the Hittite armies was next to nothing. Instead of being cautious and approaching the situation warily, he was impatient and reckless. Anticipating the battle to be short and victorious, he took the Amon division with him and told them to prepare for a siege. He and the troops camped outside of Kadesh. His intelligence, two Hittite "deserters", informed him the Hittite army and Muwatalli were at Aleppo, 100 miles distant.

Expecting a siege, the Amon division was unprepared to fight a battle. The supposed deserters deliberately divulged misinformation regarding the armies of the Hittites; they were really very close, just on the north side of Kadesh. Ramses' remaining three divisions, named Ptah, Sutech, and Re, were on the march.

Muwatalli split his army, sending half across the Orontes river to attack the Re army. The Hittites were undetected and launched a surprise attack on the flank. The Re division was decimated. The Hittite army moved northward, hoping to catch Ramses and the Amon division unaware.

Ramses was clueless that his Re division had been felled. Muwatalli hid his army in the woods surrounding the Amon division and Ramses so that Ramses would have no early warning. Unfortunately, a group of Hittite scouts were captured by the patrolling Egyptian soldiers. After being beaten for hours, the scouts admitted the Hittite army was close to the Egyptian encampment. Ramses was so surprised to hear this news that he hesitated. He did not muster his troops or prepare appropriately for the battle. He moved too slowly to mount an effective response to the intelligence. Ramses had the presence of mind to send a courier ordering the Ptah division to return to the encampment for support, but the Hittites were already moving in for the attack.

The Hittites started the battle with the chariot brigade. They were almost successful in defeating the Egyptians right then and there but the Egyptians created a barrier with their shields. The chariots pierced through the barricade and the Hittites made significant gains, rushing the Egyptians and shattering the line of troops.

While they were dominating the battle and pushing the Egyptians into a hole to destroy them and capture the pharaoh, the Hittites made their strategic error. The Hittites left the chariots to fight hand-to-hand, and then to plunder the spoils of the camp.

It was during the looting that the Ptah division surprised the unsuspecting Hittites. The Hittites received casualties so they quickly retreated to the borders of Kadesh. The next day the battle continued, but it ended in a draw between the two empires. Neither army was completely eradicated and both were allowed to limp back to their homeland.

Muwatalli could not move his infantry across the barrier of the Brook El-Mukadiyeh River, surrounded himself with a protective security force, and fought only with his chariots. Ramses claimed the victory and called Muwatalli a coward for not leading the battle, stating he had personally performed many acts of bravery as the leading commander of his troops.

Because his army was not annihilated, Ramses carved his victory into monuments, and declared that he had won the battle. The Pharaoh escaped and returned to Egypt. His campaign to conquer Syria failed.

Kadesh was still under the Kingdom of the Hittites, the Hittite military was still in full force having incurred very few casualties, and the Egyptians had retreated. Muwatalli felt that he had won. Amurru was reclaimed by the Hittites and one of his sons was named prince of Amurru. States that were moving towards a rebellion of the Hittite government backed down from their discord, remaining within the Hittite control.

There were no more conflicts or engagements between the Hittites and the Egyptians until the enemy of both empires, the Assyrians, came calling at the borders.

Mursilli III

Muwatalli II was followed by his son Mursilli III. Mursilli III had a short reign of five years. He was followed by Muwatalli II's brother, Hatusilli III.

Hatusilli III

Hatusilli III signed the world's first international peace treaty, the Treaty of Kadesh, written in 1258 B.C.E. between the Egyptians and Hittites. The peace treaty was an agreement to unite their forces against the Assyrians and the new enemy, the Sea Peoples.

When Hatusilli III died, his kingdom passed to Tudhaliya IV, his son.

Tudhaliya IV

The Assyrians attacked the Hittites at the Battle of Nihriya, and defeated the Hittites. This began the fall of the Hittite Empire. After multiple attacks from the Sea Peoples, the Hittites never regained their former strength or their territories.

Suppiluliuma II

Suppiluliuma II served as the last king of the Hittites. His victory in the first naval battle of recorded history, where the Hittite fleet conquered the Cypriots, was one of his few successes. The Sea Peoples and the Kaska tribe whittled away at the border defenses until the Hittite Empire fell apart.

The Kaskas sacked Hattus and burned it to the ground in 1190 B.C.E. Suppiluliuma II perished in this battle.

The peak of the Hittites was during the reign of Suppiluliuma I, and, ironically, the collapse of the Hittites came with the reign of Suppiluliuma II.

Chapter 6:
The Hittites and the Iron Age

The Hittites are credited with concluding the Bronze Age to usher in the Iron Age. It is problematic to date the exact year that one era ended and another began, because differing metals were used across the world. What is known regarding the Iron Age is the weapons that were used by the Hittites in battle were iron, and they were a determining factor in the expansion of the Hittite Empire.

Iron, copper, and tin were the metals involved in making tools and weapons. Tin may have been the first metal to be tempered as it has a much lower melting point than iron or copper. Tin melts at 422 degrees Fahrenheit, an easy temperature to reach and consistently maintain. Historical documents state it was first tempered in the Zagros Mountains. We don't know if the trade moved west or developed independently, but tin mining in Anatolia was discovered at approximately the same time.

In a very small village in the Taurus Mountains, a tin mine was excavated into the mountain by the citizens of Goltepe. They built more than a mile of tunnels into the mountains to obtain the tin ore. To collect the tin ore, the Goltepe miners would heat the ore while it was still in the wall. Tin is amalgamated with charcoal, so the charcoal provided the fuel for the heat. A reed pipe was used for bellows. When the tin was softened, the miners would chisel the ore into pieces to be gathered for the next phase.

Tin in itself was useful, but bronze was produced with the addition of tin to copper. Bronze was used to make strong weapons and utensils, but would not consistently hold a sharp edge. During battle the soldiers had to stop fighting to sharpen the points of their weapons, which was detrimental to their fighting abilities. Bronze also wasn't very durable.

The Hittites discovered the process of smelting iron, but it was never in mass production. One king of the Hittites, 13 B.C.E., sent a dagger fashioned of iron to another king as an apology when the king requested a supply of iron for his weaponry. It was explained the quantity requested was impossible to produce because it would take a very long time.

Iron was used to shape weapons, and to provide shields for defense. Iron was also used to make plows, which could cut much deeper into the soil than tin. The iron plow produced a field that grew a bigger yield, which gave the Hittites more grain with which to trade.

Iron was responsible for making the Hittites a formidable enemy; they had better weapons that needed less repair, they had chariots that carried three people and had iron spokes, and they had a surplus of grains so that they were wealthy in trade.

Chapter 7:
The Legacy of the Hittites

The Hittites contributed to the development of civilization in many positive ways.

The Hittite kings and queens were documented as being fair and just. They developed laws that protected the people from the wrath of the king.

When a country was conquered, the Hittites incorporated their culture and practices as a kinsfolk, instead of as a slave. They allowed the conquered people to work as serfs, which meant they had a wage. Serfs worked the land, cared for the animals, and performed the maintenance on the property. In return, the serfs were provided clothing and shelter, and given a small piece of land to work for themselves. They were allowed to keep the gleanings from their private piece of land, and even sell them in the market.

The Hittites wrote many peace treaties and worked first with compromise and mediation, negotiating their way through as many conflicts as they could. They were known as peacemakers, very humane and fair. For example, when attempting a takeover of another kingdom, the Hittites would first send an ambassador that would offer the king terms of a surrender. If the king agreed, then the king could keep the kingdom but had to accept the relationship of vassal state. If the king did not surrender, then military force was employed.

They worked for a conciliatory relationship with their trade partners. They would not trade with a kingdom that had social and political infighting.

They developed their own form of language (cuneiform) and faithfully recorded their history in massive detail. They also recorded surrounding events, like the Trojan War.

They were brilliant businessmen, using tactics that could use in modern society. They have written records of loans and contracts between parties.

They established the practice of restitution when a person lost a valuable item. If the perpetrator of the crime had died, the family was responsible for the debt.

They had a regulated economy with a set wage, prices for commodities, and property rights. The law set the price for the rental of animals or labor, in addition to the maximum amount that could be charged for trade items.

Agriculture was the basis of the local economy, along with animal husbandry.

They kept sheep, sheared the wool, and wove blankets and garments. The surplus of these products was traded to other kingdoms.

The military conquests were required to pay an annual tribute, which was used to support the standing army through payments and maintenance.

The Empire had deposits of tin, iron, copper, silver, gold, and lead, which was also used for trade with other kingdoms.

The Hittites employed trade embargos in negotiations for peace with the surrounding countries.

The Hittites introduced chariots with a team of horses. Wagons pulled by oxen can reach the speed of 2 mph, whereas a chariot with a team of horses can run at the speed of 10 mph.

The Hittites used the shekel for their currency, theirs was made of silver, but also created a coin that was stamped and made of lead.

The Hittites were renowned horsemen. They trained horses and wrote manuals about how to care for a horse. The oldest surviving book (tablet) on horse training was written by the Royal Stable Master of the Hittites.

Hittites used the oil of the soapwort plant combined with water for bathing.

The city walls built by the Hittites were tall and thick, made with a mixture very similar to concrete. Every 35 feet they built a watchtower that was manned. They had an inner wall and an outer wall around the city. There were tunnels within the walls and compartments for storage of weapons. A soldier could pass out of the city through the tunnels and never been seen.

The city of Hattusa had a water management system. They built pipes to run water from the streams in the hills and down into the city walls, where they landed in pools. There were seven pools to provide fresh water for the needs of the people.

They had an incessant thirst for knowledge preserving not only their history and chronicles, but also the correspondence of all their contemporaries, including the Trojans. There are letters discussing the Trojan Wars between the two kings.

Their soldiers were allowed to choose between drawing a salary and drawing a monetary percentage of the spoils when they captured a city-state. In essence, they could be paid on salary or commission.

They engaged in chemical warfare. When they invaded a country, they brought sheep infected with rabbit fever, which would spread to all the livestock and humans. At the time, rabbit fever had no known cure. Even today, without quick intervention, rabbit fever can produce death in humans. There is no vaccine available for Tularemia (rabbit fever.)

Chapter 8:
Hittite Society

The Hittite Society was a hybrid mix of a piece of every conquered nation and people. As the Hittites moved through territories they adapted and incorporated the local culture and practices into their society. Instead of requiring a rigid adherence to the "Hittite way" of doing things, the Hittites welcomed change and inclusiveness.

Government

As with the traditions of the Bronze Age, the King was the governing authority of the kingdom.

When a king was deposed, chaos ensued. There were riots, rebellions, and the interference of the nobles, who wanted to protect their own interests in light of a new political power. There were many collusions and even a concentration of nobles called the Assembly, whose function was to be a court of appeal, in reality, it was a group that acted in opposition to the king.

There was no line of succession from the ending of one king to the beginning of another. Interested nobles would back whichever prince would support their financial endeavors. There could be seven or eight princes all vying for the reign of the kingdom.

King Telipinus issued an edict that delineated clear rights of succession. This changed the entire political climate of the Hittites, creating a stable environment and dissolving the Assembly and the influence of the nobles.

The titles of the king changed as the kingdom evolved. In the Old Kingdom, the king was overlord of the lesser kings, so his title was "Great King." Later, due to the influence of the kings of Egypt and Syria, he became "My Sun." This changed his status from first among his peers to an absolute monarch. Kings were not considered gods while they were living, but they were believed to become gods after their death.

Administration

The kingdom of the Hittites was comprised of a homeland in Hattusa, surrounded by city-state kingdoms that served at the will of the current King.

Each town and city-state had a local council made of esteemed community members and elders. The local council took care of the problems of the community and reported to the Hittite governor or military overseer.

As the empire increased, the conquered kingdoms were incorporated into the Hittite rule. If the king had surrendered, he was usually allowed to keep his kingdom, but became a vassal state. If the king rallied his troops and fought the Hittites, the city was overtaken, often destroyed, and the citizens taken to Hattusa, along with their cattle. The citizens would be divided among the nobles to perform as serfs, but not slaves. The conquered kingdom was usually assigned to a prince for management.

The vassal state had both rights and responsibilities. The vassals supplied troops and paid a tribute to the kingdom of the Hittites. In exchange for their allegiance, the king defended them from their enemies and supported the royal family in power. Vassal kingdoms could not individually negotiate with foreign powers.

Law

The Hittites were very attentive to the legal system. They developed a code of laws that numbered more than 200, to identify the rights and privileges of a citizen of the Empire.

The laws regulated revenge and compensatory matters regarding crimes. The only offenses that involved capital punishment were rape, sexual relations with animals, and treason. Slaves did not have the same protections as they could be punished to death for sorcery and disobedience to their masters. Any crimes and misdemeanors committed by slaves were to be decided by the courts, instead of the slave owner.

Restitution was required by citizens for property that was destroyed or stolen. The compensation was figured at several times the actual value of the damages. The family and community of the perpetrator could be held responsible for the crime, financially and sometimes paying with their lives. The king's presence was required for cases of sorcery, large thefts, and the death penalty.

Women had equal rights under Hittite law on many occasions. Women commanded as queens, signed treaties, and wrote laws. A married woman had the right to be considered in marriages, and could control her dowry. If a wife died, her husband was only entitled to her possessions if they shared the same residence.

Slaves were protected in various, most notably in the case of marriage. A marriage between two partners, either of which or both that were slaves, was recognized by the courts.

Warfare

The Hittite army created the three-man horse-drawn chariot; their fighting skills with horses and chariots were superior to all the other nations, and a primary reason their expansion was so successful. The chariots were the main purveyor in a battle.

The military campaigns usually happened in the spring and summer, due to climatic changes. The military strategies of the Hittites were sophisticated and cunning. They used feints, counter marches, marches, and concealment to confuse the enemy. Their expertise with a chariot was dominant in the battle, the enemies' best defense was hand-to-hand guerrilla warfare.

The weapons of the Hittite soldiers included spears, bows, lances, short swords, and shields, all made of iron, which was another huge advantage for the Hittites. Other kingdoms had weapons made of bronze, copper, and tin. The Hittites employed battering rams for a siege. The rams were made of large timbers that had been sharpened to a point, and hung from ropes on a wheeled frame to increase the momentum of the weapon.

The Hittites were very humane in their dealings with their enemies. They did not torture or maim their captives and they did not allow them to become slaves.

Economy

Silver was the form of currency, which could be bars or rings, measured by weight, in shekels and mina. The maximum price of goods or services was set by the law to ensure economic stability and fair trade. The Hittite Empire had its own coinage that was stamped with the seal of the empire.

Religion

The religion of the Hittites was polytheistic by nature. The weather god was the most important figure, in the Hittite pantheon that was first the Sun goddess, the deity of the kings and for battle. The Storm god was her consort, and also the god of battle.

The Hittites incorporated the religious practices of each of the subject people, maintaining the shrines and ceremonies. The king was the chief priest, and had specific religious duties. Every year he visited four important shrines within the kingdom, and held religious ceremonies. The Hittite places of worship could be an open-air sanctuary or a large temple.

Magic and divination were the means by which the Hittites anticipated the will of the gods. Sorcery and black magic were a crime in Hittite law and punishable by death.

Because of the practice of incorporation of gods from all cultures, the Hittite pantheon was called the "1000 gods of Hatti." The gods were listed genealogically according to the function and strength. They were attributed with human characteristics and emotions but could appear as animals or objects. This was in keeping with their belief that all beings had a Divine Spirit.

The Hittites had a title for each god, but believed the gods had a heavenly title or name revealed only to the other gods. Hebut was the Sun Goddess and Teshuba, his consort, the Storm God. All gods were considered peers, whether they were derived from the Babylonian, Roman, Egyptian, or any number of other cultures, including the Hittites.

Language and writing

The Hittites used two languages for the official documents, Akkadian and Hittite, and one for trades and commercial transactions, Hurrian. The Hittites recorded in two scripts, hieroglyphic Hittite and cuneiform.

Art

Art in the Hittite kingdom varied. The Old Kingdom produced hand-made pottery, and decorated them with geometric designs.

Metals were used for all utensils and decorative objects like jewelry. Gemstones were incorporated into the design of headdresses and necklaces, bracelets, etc.

There were many stone bas-reliefs that provide scenes of the king or the priests performing official duties. There is one that shows a religious procession complete with jugglers, someone playing a lute, another playing bagpipes, attesting to the wide diversity of the Hittite culture.

Literature

Hittite literature is a wide assortment of songs, hymns, royal decrees, creation stories, myths, deeds, curses, treaties, and charters. The story of Gilgamesh was preserved in their literature, as well as Hesiod's Creation Story.

The most impressive literature produced by the Hittites were the vast and enormous collection of personal letters written by the kings to other contemporaries. These letters present important details of strategies and personal thoughts, a rare glimpse of the internal musings of the king. Many of the whys of history are reflected in these letters, for example Hattusilis wrote about why he chose a particular prince to rule each kingdom.

Chapter 9:
Hittite Timeline

4,000 B.C.E.   The Hittites were noted as a settlement located in present-day Cappadocia.

2,000 B.C.E.   The Hittites mixed with the Hatti.

1700 B.C.E.-1250 B.C.E.   Troy VI, the site of the Trojan War, was inhabited. The populace spoke Luvian, a language similar to Hittite.

1595 B.C.E.   The Hittites captured Babylon but then left it to the Kassites.

1450 B.C.E.-1300 B.C.E.   The Hittite culture reached its peak. They have developed their own pantheon and religion.

1350 B.C.E.   The plague of Egypt, the first recorded smallpox epidemic, was transferred to the Hittite kingdom and lasted 20 years. The population was reduced considerably and the King and his successor son died from the plague.

1347 B.C.E.-1338 B.C.E.   King Tutankhamun of Egypt, was the king for nine years before he died of an infection.

1295 B.C.E.-1272 B.C.E.   The Hittite king, Muwatalli II, wrote a treaty with King Alaksandu, ruler of the Wilusa, which was the site of Ilios for Homer's Iliad.

1286 B.C.E.   The Hittites began fighting with Egypt.

1285 B.C.E.   Battle of Kadesh, the epic battle between Ramses and Muwatallis, lasted two days. There were as many as 100,000 soldiers fighting, the largest battle in the history of the Ancient World. Egypt claimed the victory because it stopped the expansion of the Hittites.

1275 B.C.E. Pharaoh Ramses II began reclaiming kingdoms from the Hittites, such as Canaan, Amarru, and Phoenicia.

1267 B.C.E. Hattusili wrested the throne from Mursili, his nephew. After Mursili was exiled he asked Ramses the Great for asylum in Egypt.

1261 B.C.E. Egypt and the Hittite kingdom wrote and recorded the first international peace treaty, called the Treaty of Kadesh.

1248 B.C.E. Pharaoh Ramses II, married King Hattusili of Hittite's daughter.

1200 B.C.E. Assyria captured the capital, Hattusa, and sacked and burned it to the ground.

1185 B.C.E. The Hittite empire fell apart and was incorporated by the "Sea People."

The Kings and their Reigns

Pithana	early 18th c.
Anitta	mid 18th c.
Labarna	1680-1650
Hattusili I	1650-1620
Mursili I	1620-1590
Hantili	1590-1560
Zidanta I	1560-1550
Ammuna	1550-1530
Huzziya I	1530-1525
Telipinu	1525-1500
Tahurwaili	
Alluwamna	
Hantili II	1500-1450
Zidanta II	
Huzziya II	
Muwatalli I	
Tudhaliya II	1450-1420
Arnuwanda I	1420-1400
Tudhaliya III	1400-1380
Tudhaliya	1380
Hattusili II	
Suppiluliuma I	1380-1340
Arnuwanda II	1340-1339

Mursili II	1339-1306
Muwatalli II	1306-1282
Mursili III	1282-1275
Hattusili III	1275-1250
Tudhaliya IV	1250-1220
Karunta	
Arnuwanda III	1220-1215
Suppiluliuma II	1215-1200

Conclusion

Thank for making it through to the end of this book, let's hope it was informative and able to provide you with all of the tools you need to achieve your goals whatever they may be.

The next step is to investigate another Ancient Empire. When comparing the successes of the early kings and governors, it is amazing to discover there is nothing new under the sun.

Finally, if you found this book useful in anyway, a review on Amazon is always appreciated!

About The Book

The Hittites, most known as the opposers of Israel in the Old Testament and the Torah, were a mystery throughout the ages until their recorded tablets were discovered in the early 1900's. The Hittites chronicled the history and major events in cuneiform onto more than 25,000 stone tablets. After discovery the key to their language translation, scholars treated to a complete description of the culture and key military conquests.

Some of the questions answered by the tablets included:

- Where did they originate?
- How did they expand their kingdom?
- Who were their notable peers?
- What were their significant accomplishments?
- What is their legacy?

In this book, we discuss these questions and more details about the life and habits of the Hittites. We narrate extensively the Battle of Kadesh, and discuss the insertion of Ramses and King Tut into the history of the Hittites.

We delineate the personal correspondence of the kings with neighboring peers, discussing important events like the Trojan War. We note the effects of the plague of Egypt on the Hittite Empire.

The kingdom of the Hittites encompassed over 4,000 square miles and rivaled Egypt and Assyria, just a few of their neighboring enemies. Their contribution to the Iron Age, the modification of the chariot, and their horse training skills have impacted civilization as a lasting tribute to their innovative spirit.

Made in United States
Orlando, FL
17 May 2024

46938864R00039